ARTIFICIAL INTELLIG

COLLECTION

IMPACTS AND TRANSFORMATIONS

VOLUME 6

THE ERA OF STUPIDITY!

A CULT OF STUPIDITY

Prof. Marcão - Marcus Vinícius Pinto

Disclaimer:

Please note that the information contained in this document is for educational and entertainment purposes only. Every effort has been made to provide complete, accurate, up-to-date, and reliable information. No warranty of any kind is express or implied.

By reading this text, the reader agrees that under no circumstances are the authors liable for any losses, direct or indirect, incurred as a result of the use of the information contained in this book, including, but not limited to, errors, omissions, or inaccuracies.

ISBN: **9798345040348**

Publishing imprint: Independently published

Summary

Welcome.

"Man is something that must be overcome. What have you done to overcome it?"
Friedrich Nietzsche[1]

We live in paradoxical times, where the availability of information has never been so vast, and the understanding so limited. "The Era of Stupidity! A Cult of Stupidity?" is an invitation to explore the dynamics behind this reality and to reflect on the cognitive pitfalls that lead us to make increasingly irrational decisions, even in a scenario of an abundance of data.

Part of the collection "Artificial Intelligence: The Power of Data", for sale on Amazon, this volume proposes a comprehensive analysis of how human failures and artificial intelligence (AI) meet, interact and sometimes amplify each other.

This book is essential reading for those seeking to understand not only the technologies that shape our world, but also the human behaviors and limitations that interfere with this progress.

Professionals in artificial intelligence, data science, digital communication, psychology, politics, and education will find, in the pages that follow, a critical analysis of the factors that contribute to collective ignorance, even in a digital age.

---

[1] Nineteenth-century German philosopher

For experts and leaders in AI and data, this book offers an in-depth reflection on the risks inherent in integrating technology in a context of human error.

By understanding biases, misinformation, and how these elements are amplified by AI systems, these professionals will be better prepared to implement technologies with more responsibility and ethics.

Communications managers and media professionals will recognize how fake news, infodemic, and technological stupidity impact public perception and opinion, while educators and psychologists will find valuable insights into the effects of constant exposure to misinformation and the breakdown of discernment.

The book offers a series of chapters that address the phenomenon of "collective stupidity" in its multiple facets. From the construction of fake news and the proliferation of disinformation to what we call technological stupidity — the inability to adapt or critically use digital tools.

In each section, concepts are explained and broken down with practical examples and tips for dealing with the challenges that the digital age imposes on us. At the end of each chapter, readers will find practical suggestions for developing a more critical relationship with technology and with information itself.

This book also provides an in-depth discussion of the infodemic, exploring the breakdown of discernment in times of informational overload.

You will see how the abundance of data, instead of making us more enlightened, generates confusion and cognitive fatigue, leading us to impulsive and irrational decisions. In times when we are bombarded by polarized content, this book invites the reader to reflect on the mechanisms of manipulation and the cognitive traps that make the digital age also the era of collective stupidity.

By reading this book, you will be able to:

- Recognize and understand the cognitive pitfalls that lead to misinformation and collective ignorance;

- Develop a critical view on the impact of artificial intelligence on a society prone to biases and fallacies;

- Identify and resist fake news, disinformation campaigns, and information bubbles;

- Understand the infodemic and how information overload contributes to cognitive exhaustion and hasty decisions;

- Integrate a more conscious and ethical approach to the use of technologies and data consumption.

"The Era of Stupidity! A Cult of Stupidity?" is more than a guide to understanding the challenges of the digital age; It is an invitation to revisit our relationship with information and technology, developing critical and reflective thinking.

However, this is just one step in an essential journey in the field of artificial intelligence. This volume is part of a larger collection, "Artificial Intelligence: The Power of Data," which explores, in depth, different aspects of AI and data science.

The other volumes address equally crucial topics, such as the integration of AI systems, predictive analytics, and the use of advanced algorithms for decision-making.

By purchasing and reading the other books in the collection, you will have a holistic and deep view that will allow you not only to optimize data governance, but also to enhance the impact of artificial intelligence on your operations, transforming your approach to the challenges and opportunities of the digital age.

Good learning!

Prof. Marcão - Marcus Vinícius Pinto

M. Sc. in Information Technology
Specialist in Information Technology.
Consultant, Mentor and Speaker on Artificial Intelligence,
Information Architecture and Data Governance.
Founder, CEO, teacher and
pedagogical advisor at MVP Consult.

1 The era of stupidity! A cult of stupidity?

A precipitous decline of civilization, marked by angry and fruitless debates. The search for truth has given way to the stubborn defense of false and polarized narratives. Intolerance, once a stain, has become the identity of many.

Disinformation spreads like a virus, eroding the pillars of society. Promising projects are sabotaged by ineptitude and lack of long-term vision.

Decision-making, once an act of responsibility, has become a game of power and personal interests.

Remembering that decision-making is a cognitive process that involves selecting an option or course of action among several alternatives. It is a central element in our daily lives, from simple choices to complex decisions that impact our lives and businesses.

This process involves evaluating, analyzing, weighing information, and considering the possible outcomes before reaching a conclusion.

1.1 Imbecile political leaders, whose actions echo the voice of ignorance and selfishness.

For some time now, it seems that the world has thrown itself headlong into an abyss of stupidity.

Have you ever had this feeling? A growing anguish in the face of the apparent insanity that unfolds around us? Perhaps it is not just a sensation, but a harsh reality that we are being forced to face.

Painstaking studies, conducted on tens of thousands of people in several countries, shed light on something as unprecedented as it is frightening: human intelligence, once celebrated as a rare jewel of evolution, appears to be in decline.

The scenario is bleak. In an age where information is abundantly accessible, we are suffocated by a vacuum of wisdom. The space that should be reserved for rational debates and exchanges of knowledge has been invaded by a horde of voices that praise the absurd and irrationality.

The ability to discern between fact and fiction fades as conspiracy theories intertwine with reality in alarming ways.

The political landscape is no less disturbing. Vital decisions are made based on momentary impulses, with no regard for long-term consequences.

Leaders who should serve as beacons of rationality seem to be more interested in immediate applause than in building a solid future. Those who crave power often rely on empty speeches that appeal to the lowest emotions, rather than proposing reasoned solutions.

1.2 How did we get to this point?

The inevitable question is: how did we get to this point? What led to this intellectual decay? Are we doomed to be spectators of our own decline?

The dangerous belief that any opinion, no matter how absurd, deserves the same weight as proven knowledge, feeds the chaos of misinformation and corrodes the pillars of society.

Umberto Eco[2], in an interview for La Stampa (2015):

---

[2] Italian intellectual, with a vast body of work covering philosophy, semiotics, literature and cultural criticism. Born in 1932, Eco became an influential figure on the world intellectual scene, especially after the resounding success of his first novel, "The Name of the Rose".

"Social networks give the right to speak to legions of imbeciles who used to speak only at the bar after a glass of wine, without harming the community. They were immediately silenced, while now they have the same right to speak as a Nobel Prize winner. It's the invasion of the imbeciles."

2   There are so few answers to so many questions!

Eugenics, with its promise to create a 'master race', has already shown us the horrors that science can commit when it puts itself at the service of ideology.

Comparing intelligence or other human characteristics as if they were currencies to be exchanged in a market is not only unhuman, but also scientifically flawed. History teaches us that genetic diversity is our greatest wealth, and any attempt to manipulate it in the name of an ideal of perfection is a path of no return to barbarism.

One hypothesis, this one developed, among others, by Mark Bauerlein, Professor at Emory University, in the United States, and author of the book "The Dumbest Generation Grows Up", would be "that the technological leap of the last 20 years, which has transformed our daily lives, may have begun to affect human intelligence."

According to Bauerlein: "today, children of 7 or 8 years old already grow up with their cell phones," precisely the period of life in which "they should consolidate the habit of reading, to acquire vocabulary."

Noting that it is not a Luddite[3], the professor says that there are indeed indications that the use of smartphones and tablets in childhood is already causing negative effects.

---

[3] The Luddites were a group of English textile workers of the early nineteenth century who were vehemently opposed to the mechanization of industry. In an era marked by the Industrial Revolution and the growing use of machines, these workers saw in new technologies a direct threat to their jobs.

In England, for example, 28% of preschool children (4 and 5 years old) do not know how to communicate using complete sentences, at the level that would be normal for this age. According to educators, this is due to the time they spend in front of TVs, tablets and smartphones.

The problem is considered so serious that the government has announced a plan to reduce this rate by half by 2028 – and banning smartphones in schools is one of the measures under discussion.

The digital revolution, with its social networks and streaming platforms, has promised to connect the world and democratize access to information. However, there is a harmful side effect in this story: the fragmentation of attention and the superficialization of knowledge.

In his book "Fatigue Society", philosopher Byung-Chul Han warns of the dangers of the culture of distraction, in which we are constantly bombarded by fragmented and superficial information.

This fragmentation, according to Han, "erodes our ability to pay attention to things." Neuroscientist Nicole LePera, in her bestseller "How to Heal Your Life", corroborates this idea by stating that excessive use of social networks can lead to decreased ability to concentrate and intensify anxiety.

The feeling that it is increasingly difficult to complete a text or a video is a symptom of a deeper disease: the fragmentation of our attention.

The culture of clicking, liking and infinite scrolling, carefully designed by the large digital platforms, alienates us from the capacity for deep reflection.

This superficiality not only prevents the construction of solid knowledge, but also makes us more vulnerable to manipulation and misinformation.

of attention is also addressed by philosopher Zygmunt Bauman, who works on the concept that we live in a liquid society, in which everything is disposable and relationships are increasingly superficial. This superficiality manifests itself in all spheres of life, from politics to culture.

The need to simplify messages to reach an increasingly fragmented audience has led to the proliferation of simplistic and polarized discourses, which hinder dialogue and consensus-building.

Woke culture, the result of the digital age and social networks, is more a symptom than a cause of the superficiality that dominates the public debate. By transforming the complexity of the world into hashtags and memes, it contributes to the fragmentation of attention and the simplification of social issues.

This tendency towards simplification, in turn, fuels polarization and intolerance, preventing the construction of a consensus around complex issues.

Superficiality is not only an individual problem, but a social problem that requires a deep reflection on the way we consume and produce information. It is essential that we develop critical thinking skills, which allow us to question the information we receive and seek reliable sources.

In addition, digital platforms need to be redesigned to encourage reflection and deepening, rather than just distraction.

3   The cult of stupidity and intolerance to the intolerant.

The rise of the cult of stupidity poses an existential threat to reason and democracy. The proliferation of fake news, political polarization, and the rise of populist leaders, all fueled by social media, have created an environment conducive to the spread of ignorance.

The algorithmic nature of digital platforms, designed to maximize engagement, prioritizes sensationalist and emotionally charged content over accurate and contextualized information.

This manipulation of the masses, combined with the devaluation of expertise, has undermined trust in institutions and experts, creating a knowledge vacuum that is quickly filled by pseudosciences and conspiracy theories.

The viralization of false information, created to attract clicks and shares, contributes to the proliferation of stupidity, moving us further and further away from the firm ground of reality.

In addition, political polarization and the fragmentation of information bubbles exacerbate the problem. The idea that "my opinion is only as valid as your knowledge" finds fertile ground in these divisions.

The rejection of critical thinking in favor of one-sided views creates an environment where ignorance is not only tolerated but also celebrated.

Anti-intellectualism is also driven by distrust in educational and scientific institutions. At a time when conspiracy theories are gaining ground and experts are often discredited, research-based knowledge is placed under suspicion.

The idea that "we all know enough" undermines the authority of educated voices, making room for the void of stupidity.

Isaac Asimov highlighted the false notion that democracy would level the playing field between ignorance and knowledge. This distorted interpretation of democracy contributes to the formation of a culture where the cult of stupidity is exalted.

How, then, to understand the apparent proliferation of stupidity even among those who attended schools?

The data from the surveys are alarming: 29% of the Brazilian adult population is functionally illiterate.

This reality, which compromises the full participation of citizens in social and political life, is aggravated by the absence of effective public policies and the devaluation of education.

The genetic justification, proposed by Michael Woodley, from the University of Umeã, in Sweden, according to which "Cognitive ability is strongly influenced by genetics.

And people with high levels of it are having fewer children" is simplistic and ignores the complex interactions between genetic and environmental factors that shape intelligence. This deterministic view only serves to justify inequality and social exclusion.

4   In the political field, this phenomenon is quite visible.

A study by Carnegie Mellon University reveals a worrying phenomenon: the infantilization of political language. The finding that American politicians, including presidents, express themselves at a level similar to that of children and adolescents is a clear sign of the declining quality of public debate.

This trend, which is not restricted to the United States, can be explained by several factors. The pressure for immediate results in the age of social networks, the need to simplify messages for an increasingly fragmented audience, and the devaluation of formal education are some of the elements that contribute to this infantilization.

The consequences of this simplification are serious. The difficulty in discussing complex ideas, the proliferation of empty speeches and political polarization are just some of the side effects. When political leaders express themselves on a childish level, democracy is weakened, as the ability to make informed decisions and build consensus becomes increasingly difficult.

The media, especially television and social networks, play a key role in this process. The search for an audience and the need to generate clicks lead to the production of increasingly simple and sensationalist content, which reinforces the tendency to infantilize political language.

The study analyzed the vocabulary and syntax of five candidates in recent presidential elections (Donald Trump, Hillary Clinton, Ted Cruz, Marco Rubio, and Bernie Sanders), and found that their pronouncements have the verbal level of an 11- to 13-year-old.

The researchers also analyzed the speeches of former American presidents, and found a steady decline. Abraham Lincoln expressed himself on the same level as a 16-year-old teenager. Ronald Reagan, 14. Obama and Clinton, 13. Trump, 11. In a last less than honorable position is George W. Bush, with the vocabulary of a 10-year-old.

While this finding is evident, it does not imply, in isolation, that politicians are becoming increasingly stupid over time. Perhaps more incompetent, but not necessarily less intelligent.

As pointed out by journalists Eduardo Szklarz and Bruno Garattoni, who wrote an article for issue no. 394, of Super Interessante Magazine, entitled "*The Age of Stupidity*"', politicians are not necessarily getting dumber. They are, in fact, being pragmatic in tailoring their messages to an audience that is increasingly alienated and willing to consume simple, sensationalized information.

This strategy, which takes advantage of our tendency to confirm our own biases, contributes to the deterioration of public debate and the spread of hate speech and disinformation.

As they themselves conclude, it is an irrational behavior, reminiscent of a well-known phenomenon in psychology, "*confirmation bias*", consisting of the fact that an irrational person always maintains "*his own opinion*", even if "*in the face of the most irrefutable arguments.*"

It's the old human tendency "*to embrace information that supports your beliefs, and reject data that contradicts it.*"

This phenomenon was studied by the American psychologist Kevin Dunbar, from Stanford University:

"There's too much information around us, and neurons need to filter it out. There is even a brain region, the dorsolateral prefrontal cortex, whose function is to suppress information that the mind considers 'unwanted'.

There's more: our brain releases a discharge of dopamine, a neurotransmitter linked to the feeling of pleasure, when we receive information that confirms our beliefs. We are programmed not to change our opinions. Even if it means believing things that aren't true."

See, among countless others, the example of the "flat-earthers."

This thing about irrationality is so serious that there are those who defend the thesis that "reason" does not really exist, at least as we conceive it. In this sense, cognitive scientists Hugo Mercier and Dan Sperber, from Harvard, in the book "*The Enigma of Reason*", state "*that reason is relative. It changes according to the context, and its great utility is to build social agreements – whatever the cost.*"

That's that!

So, apart from the fascists, there are, to make matters worse! the dumb and the irrational.

---

5 Human intelligence versus artificial intelligence: encounter, conflict and cooperation.

In a world increasingly shaped by the presence of artificial intelligence (AI), an essential question emerges: how does this form of intelligence differ from the one that characterizes the human mind?

Understanding the difference between human and artificial intelligence is more than a theoretical issue; It is an analysis with profound practical implications, which affects our personal, economic and social choices.

Human intelligence, with its capacities for adaptation, intuition, and creativity, and artificial intelligence, with its speed, precision, and ability to process at scale, form a complex interaction, whose unfolding is both fascinating and unsettling.

To navigate this new technological era, we need to understand how these two forms of intelligence relate to each other, where they complement each other, and where they inevitably collide.

5.1 Human intelligence: adaptability and subjectivity.

Human intelligence is characterized by adaptability, the ability to learn from a wide variety of experiences, and the ability to interpret the world with an emotional and subjective bias.

Since ancient civilizations, this intelligence has been fundamental for human survival and progress, allowing the creation of cultures, the resolution of complex problems, and the development of ethical and justice systems.

Human intelligence, however, is limited by subjectivity and emotional biases.

Our decisions are often guided by personal experiences, perceptions, and even cognitive fallacies, such as confirmation bias, which leads us to value information that corroborates our preexisting beliefs, ignoring contrary data.

This is particularly relevant in the context of AI, as artificial intelligence, on the contrary, seeks to operate with objectivity and numerical precision.

Example: decisions in the medical field.

In the field of medicine, human subjectivity is both a force and a limitation. Doctors and healthcare professionals often make complex decisions based not only on data, but also on intuition, accumulated experience, and clinical judgment. However, these decisions are subject to bias.

A study published by the British Medical Journal revealed that doctors tend to overestimate the severity of illnesses in patients who demonstrate symptoms of anxiety, which can lead to unnecessary treatments or misdiagnoses.

Here, artificial intelligence comes in as a complementary tool. AI systems, such as IBM Watson Health, are capable of analyzing vast medical databases, offering diagnoses based on statistical evidence.

However, this accuracy is not foolproof: without human expertise, AI can overlook important nuances in a patient's clinical picture. Therefore, the complementarity between human intelligence and AI proves to be crucial, as an optimal decision requires both objective analysis and subjective interpretation.

5.2   Artificial intelligence: processing power and cognitive limitations

Artificial intelligence is defined by its ability to process large volumes of data at extreme speed, identify patterns, and optimize solutions to specific problems.

Unlike human intelligence, AI has no emotions, biases, or interests of its own; His "thinking" is linear, analytical, and guided exclusively by data and algorithms.

While this makes it extremely effective in various areas, such as medical diagnostics, image recognition, and language processing, AI also faces limitations.

AI is programmed to solve problems within defined parameters; He does not have genuine creativity, nor the ability to form abstract concepts or to apply knowledge in contexts outside those for which he was trained. These limits highlight the importance of maintaining human oversight in critical processes involving AI.

Example: recruitment algorithms and their biases.

An application of AI in talent recruitment has revealed an important paradox. Tech companies, such as Amazon, have used AI algorithms to sift through resumes and streamline the hiring process.

However, the system demonstrated a bias against female candidates. This bias arose because the algorithm was trained based on historical data from predominantly male resumes, leading it to prefer characteristics associated with male profiles.

This example reveals a crucial limitation: AI, while efficient at analyzing patterns, reflects the biases of the data on which it has been trained. Without human adjustment and an ethical review of data, these systems can perpetuate biases and amplify inequalities.

5.3 Behavioral patterns and emotional capacity: the human side of intelligence.

Human intelligence is also defined by the ability to experience and interpret emotions, something that AI cannot yet replicate. Empathy, for example, is a uniquely human skill that plays a key role in professions that require interpersonal relationships, such as teaching, healthcare, and leadership.

AI, as sophisticated as it is, still operates without a real understanding of the emotional significance of human interactions, which makes it limited in fields where emotional sensitivity is required.

Example: AI and customer service.

Customer service is one area where artificial intelligence has been widely adopted. AI chatbots, such as Zendesk AI Chat, are efficient at answering common questions, offering quick support, and often improving the customer experience.

However, when service requires empathy — such as in situations where the customer expresses frustration or deep dissatisfaction — AI has limitations.

The inability to recognize the emotional tone and respond with compassion can result in an unsatisfactory user experience, leading companies to opt for a hybrid approach, where AI is used for simpler tasks, while human agents respond to more emotionally complex cases.

5.4 Creativity and adaptation: limits and possibilities.

One of the most striking differences between human and artificial intelligence is in the ability to create and adapt. Creativity is a manifestation of human intelligence that defies logic and purely algorithmic training, as it involves combining seemingly unconnected ideas to generate something new and original.

AI, despite being able to reproduce creative patterns from data and create art based on algorithms, still lacks genuine creativity, as it lacks the subjectivity and life experience that fuel human innovation.

Example: AI in art production.

In recent years, we've seen AI venture into the field of the arts, with systems like OpenAI's DALL-E generating images from textual descriptions.

The AI is capable of analyzing thousands of artworks and generating images based on stylistic patterns, which is impressive. However, this "creativity" is limited to data that AI already knows; it is not capable of creating something entirely new, as it lacks the emotional and cultural baggage that guides human artists.

Human artistic creation is, to a large extent, a reflection of subjective experiences and a search for meaning that goes beyond standards. While AI can mimic these expressions, the depth of a creative process remains unique to humans, highlighting the fundamental limitation of AI in contexts of radical innovation.

5.5   Tips for harmonizing human and artificial intelligence.

1   Complementarity of decisions: In fields such as healthcare and recruitment, use AI as a support, but maintain human oversight. This prevents algorithmic biases from consolidating and ensures a more comprehensive evaluation.

2   Critical review of data: It is essential to review the data that feeds AI systems by identifying potential biases before their implementation. This is especially important in areas where decisions tend to affect individual rights and opportunities, such as recruitment.

3   Education for critical and ethical thinking: AI professionals and users should be trained not only in technical skills, but also in critical and ethical thinking, to question and adjust algorithmic decisions as needed.

4   Adopting hybrid models: Whenever possible, implement hybrid systems that harness the power of AI but with human support to validate and review decisions in areas that require empathy and contextual analysis.

6 Infodemic: because the abundance of information feeds collective stupidity.

The digital age, characterized by the almost unlimited abundance of information, has placed us in front of an unsettling paradox: the more data we have at our disposal, the more evident the presence of a "growing stupidity" in different areas of society becomes.

This phenomenon, in which the infodemic — the often conflicting and low-quality overload of information — contributes to disinformation, raises the question: how can the abundance of information feed ignorance instead of wisdom?

To understand this dynamic, it is necessary to consider some key factors. First, the infodemic creates a scenario where discernment becomes increasingly difficult.

With so much information available, there is a dilution of quality and reliability. Not everyone has the tools or patience to differentiate reliable sources from dubious sources, which results in the uncritical adoption of misinformation.

In other words, too much data, rather than enriching us, confuses and disperses our attention, often feeding preexisting biases rather than fostering deep, grounded understanding.

In addition, the proliferation of confirmation biases is exacerbated by algorithms that personalize the flow of information based on our preferences and previous interactions.

These systems, present on social networks and search engines, filter the content we view, reinforcing ideas with which we already agree and obscuring contrary views.

Rather than broadening the cognitive horizon, this algorithmic filter creates "echo chambers" where individual beliefs are reinforced, while other perspectives are ignored.

The consequence of this is a kind of "self-stupidity," in which people become increasingly confident in their worldviews, without realizing that they are moving away from the complexity and diversity of thought necessary for true understanding.

Another factor that drives stupidity in times of infodemic is cognitive exhaustion. The massive amount of data we are exposed to on a daily basis leads to mental overload.

People, when confronted with this volume of information, resort to mental shortcuts and heuristics — quick and intuitive solutions that help deal with overstimuli, but which often lead to simplistic or erroneous judgments.

These automatic decisions, often driven by emotion or fatigue, aggravate the superficiality with which we assimilate and react to information.

Another relevant aspect is the role of sensationalist and polarizing information, which tends to be more attractive and capture the public's attention, generating quick and intense reactions.

This information, widely promoted by algorithms that prioritize engagement, becomes a disseminator of simplified and emotionally charged ideas.

Thus, instead of promoting critical analysis and reasoned debate, the infodemic transforms information into a fast-paced and polarizing consumer product, encouraging short-sighted and extremist judgments. The public, immersed in a continuous flow of emotionally charged content, adopts more reactive and less reflective postures, which contributes to the strengthening of collective stupidity.

In short, the infodemic transforms information overload into a source of disinformation and stupidity, creating a scenario where superficiality and conformism replace critical analysis and reflection.

The challenge we face, therefore, is to develop skills and tools that allow us to navigate this ocean of data with discernment, favoring a critical and conscious approach to information.

7 Fake news, disinformation, technological stupidity and infodemic: a critical analysis of the challenges of the digital age.

In recent years, terms such as fake news, disinformation, technological stupidity, and infodemic have emerged as keywords to describe the complex dynamics of our connected society.

Each of these concepts represents a distinct but interconnected dimension of the problems we face in the digital age. Although they are often used interchangeably, they have fundamental differences that are worth analyzing and understanding in depth.

7.1 Fake news: the factory of alternative truths

The concept of fake news refers to false or misleading information that is deliberately fabricated to resemble real news.

This information is created with the intention of deceiving, influencing opinions or even provoking social divisions. Fake news often addresses sensitive topics and appeals to the emotional, using sensationalist titles and provocative narratives to generate engagement and rapid dissemination.

A classic example of fake news occurred in the 2016 U.S. presidential election, when false reporting about candidates and policies was widely shared on social media, potentially influencing millions of voters.

During the campaign, stories like the "Pizzagate" theory, which alleged that Hillary Clinton was involved in a child trafficking ring organized in a pizzeria, spread like wildfire, leading people to take irrational actions based on lies.

Fake news exploits human biases, such as confirmation bias (the tendency to accept information that reinforces preexisting beliefs) and availability heuristics (the tendency to judge the likelihood of an event based on how easily it is remembered).

In the digital environment, social media platforms, fed by algorithms that prioritize engagement, amplify the reach of fake news, generating a cycle of disinformation.

7.2   Combating Fake News.

To avoid falling into the traps of fake news, the reader can adopt a critical stance when consuming information online. It is recommended to always verify the source of the news by looking for independent and verified sources.

In addition, fact-checking tools, such as Aos Fatos and FactCheck.org, can be valuable resources to confirm the veracity of information.

7.3   Disinformation: intentional manipulation of opinions.

Although disinformation shares similarities with fake news, it has distinct nuances. Disinformation refers to false or misleading information that is disseminated for the purpose of manipulating opinions and controlling narratives, but it does not always have to pass itself off as a news story.

Often, misinformation is subtle and involves the omission of certain facts or the exaggeration of others, with the aim of influencing perceptions in a covert way.

A notorious example of disinformation is the use of bots and fake profiles on social networks to spread polarizing content.

During the Brexit referendum in the United Kingdom, automated accounts were used to disseminate misleading data about the consequences of remaining in or leaving the European bloc, influencing voting behavior based on half-truths and data distortions.

Here, disinformation acts as a weapon to manipulate public opinion, exploiting the inability of many to distinguish between facts and manipulated opinions.

7.4   Identification and resistance to misinformation.

To avoid being manipulated by misinformation, the reader must develop critical thinking and source analysis skills. Distrusting information that promotes strong emotional responses, such as fear or anger, can be an indicator of manipulation.

Additionally, comparing news and information from different reliable sources helps to identify discrepancies and avoid the effect of a single biased perspective.

7.5   Technological stupidity: the inability to critically use technology.

Technological stupidity is a concept that describes the inability of individuals or groups to use technology in a critical and informed way.

Technological stupidity can manifest itself in the form of both technological rejection and blind submission.

Rejection occurs when individuals or institutions resist adopting essential technologies, often due to a limited understanding of what these tools can offer.

Blind submission, on the other hand, occurs when people use technology without questioning its limitations, relying unrestrictedly on algorithms and automated systems.

A real example of technological stupidity can be found in the indiscriminate adoption of facial recognition algorithms in public security systems, without considering the possible biases and ethical failures involved.

Studies have revealed that these systems often have misidentification, especially in racial minorities and in women. Without a critical understanding of these limitations, society risks accepting technological injustices and discriminations as part of the "normal" innovation process.

7.6   Practical tip: overcoming technological stupidity.

To avoid technological stupidity, it is essential that people understand the basics of the tools they use.

Attending introductory courses on technology and AI, as well as following reliable sources that analyze and discuss technological advancements, can help develop a more critical view.

Digital education is essential for technology to be used ethically and consciously.

7.7   Infodemic: the collapse of discernment in times of information abundance.

The term infodemic describes the overload of information, usually of varying quality, that confuses rather than clarifies.

In the digital age, unlimited access to data sounds promising, but it quickly becomes a problem when there are no filters or adequate tools to differentiate relevant information from noise.

The infodemic causes cognitive exhaustion, where people, when exposed to an excess of data, find it difficult to distinguish what is true from what is false or irrelevant.

An example of an infodemic was the circulation of contradictory and confusing information during the COVID-19 pandemic.

Due to the massive amount of information — often conflicting — about the virus, treatments, and preventive measures, the general public has become disoriented, which has contributed to the rise of conspiracy theories and false information about the disease.

Here, the infodemic has turned into an obstacle to public health, where people have stopped trusting official sources due to the bombardment of incoherent information.

7.8   Navigating the infodemic

To deal with the infodemic, it is important to practice curating information. Selecting a few reliable sources and limiting the amount of information consumed helps reduce cognitive overload.

In addition, the use of verified sources, such as official bodies and scientific publications, can contribute to a clearer and more objective understanding of complex topics.

7.9   Interconnections and social implications: the cycle of digital ignorance

These four concepts — fake news, disinformation, technological stupidity, and infodemic — do not operate in isolation. They form a feedback loop, where each of the elements reinforces the other.

The proliferation of fake news and disinformation intensifies the infodemic, while technological stupidity makes it difficult for many individuals to discern reliable information. Together, these dynamics create an environment where ignorance not only persists but expands.

Ultimately, the digital age requires new and complex critical thinking and analytical skills so that we can navigate this sea of data and information in a healthy and productive way.

Without these skills, we are destined to perpetuate a cycle of disinformation and manipulation, in which the abundance of information turns into a source of ignorance and manipulation.

8   The Degeneration of Human IQ: Cognitive Decline in the Age of the Cult of Stupidity.

In recent decades, the IQ (Intelligence Quotient) index, a metric commonly used to assess cognitive abilities such as logical reasoning, memory, and comprehension, has become the subject of great debate.

Most modern studies indicate that human IQ has been declining in several developed countries, especially since the end of the twentieth century.

This phenomenon, surprising and paradoxical in an era marked by technological advances and easy access to information, suggests that we are facing a process of cognitive degeneration.

In a context in which society seems to worship ignorance, this trend takes on worrying characteristics and raises questions about the impacts of factors such as education, technology, and mass culture.

8.1   The decline of IQ: cultural and environmental factors.

Studies in countries such as Norway and France point to a downward trend in IQ indices, especially in more recent generations.

Research led by Bratsberg and Rogeberg, published in the scientific journal Proceedings of the National Academy of Sciences, concluded that the Norwegian average IQ began to decline consistently after the 1970s.

This data contradicts the so-called Flynn effect — the trend of increasing IQ over the course of the twentieth century, associated with improvements in nutrition, education and public health.

The main question that arises is: why, even in an era of progress and informational abundance, are we facing a drop in cognitive capacities?

Many researchers argue that environmental, social, and cultural factors play a crucial role in this decline.

Continuous exposure to simplistic and superficial content, the excessive use of technological devices, and the encouragement of a culture of quick and thoughtless consumption are elements that contribute to the degeneration of human IQ.

8.2   Education and superficiality of content.

Education, which should be the main pillar of intellectual development, has become one of the areas most affected by the culture of superficiality.

In many countries, education policies promote "automatic passing," where students pass regardless of their performance, and curricula are tailored to facilitate passing standardized exams rather than encouraging critical thinking.

This system creates a society of "empty knowledge," where deep learning is replaced by superficial memorization.

To reverse this trend, it is crucial that educational systems value intellectual curiosity and analytical thinking rather than just stimulating the reproduction of information.

Schools that integrate investigative activities, debates, and critical analysis of complex topics in their disciplines demonstrate a positive impact on students' cognitive development.

Finland, for example, is known for its education system that values depth of learning and curiosity, which contributes to the development of more robust cognitive skills.

8.3   The culture of distraction: how technology affects reasoning.

Another relevant factor in the degeneration of IQ is the impact of digital technology and, particularly, social networks and mobile devices.

The attention economy — the economic model that underpins many digital platforms — is based on keeping users connected for as long as possible, which results in a constant consumption of short, fast, and emotionally charged content.

This type of consumption negatively impacts our ability to concentrate, analyze and even empathize.

8.4   The effect of social networks on cognitive behavior.

Research conducted by psychologist Larry Rosen indicates that constant use of social networks is associated with a decrease in concentration skills and an increase in anxiety levels, affecting cognitive performance.

These digital environments fragment attention and create a constant state of superficial stimulation, where users are encouraged to consume and react quickly, with no time for reflection.

To mitigate these effects, it is recommended to adopt digital hygiene practices, which include limiting the time spent using social networks, practicing in-depth reading of books and scientific articles, and incorporating moments of reflection and digital pause into everyday life.

Time tracking tools on devices, such as Apple's Screen Time, help track the time spent on each app and can be a first step towards a more balanced approach to technology.

8.5   Collective stupidity and the cycle of algorithmic self-affirmation.

The digital age also contributes to the formation of "echo chambers", where recommendation algorithms, used on social networks and search platforms, continuously reinforce users' existing opinions and preferences.

Instead of exposing people to new ideas and promoting intellectual growth, algorithms fuel a cycle of self-affirmation, where users are encouraged to consume information that confirms their beliefs, rather than challenge them.

8.6   The youtube algorithm and the formation of polarized opinions.

A study conducted by The Wall Street Journal revealed that YouTube's algorithm often suggests extremist and polarized content, encouraging users to consume increasingly radical content.

This phenomenon is a demonstration of how technology can promote collective stupidity, creating homogeneous groups where critical reasoning and openness to different perspectives are stifled.

To avoid the formation of echo chambers, it is recommended to actively seek content from varied sources and verify information from different perspectives. Reading journals with divergent editorial lines and dialoguing with people with opposing opinions are practices that help to break with the effects of algorithmic self-assertion.

8.7   The impact of disinformation and fake news on collective intelligence.

Disinformation and fake news are now one of the main threats to collective intelligence and the ability to make informed decisions.

The consumption of fake news not only distorts the perception of reality, but also weakens the capacity for critical reasoning.

A population that bases its decisions on erroneous information compromises its ability to deal with complex challenges, being more susceptible to manipulation.

8.8   Fake news in public health.

During the COVID-19 pandemic, the spread of false information about treatments and vaccines led millions of people to harmful health decisions, which negatively impacted policies to contain the virus.

This example illustrates how misinformation can compromise collective thinking and exacerbate collective stupidity on a global scale.

Fact-checking is an essential practice to avoid the influence of misinformation.

Consulting reliable sources, such as public health organizations, newspapers with historical credibility, and fact-checking tools, helps prevent the spread of false information and protects collective intelligence.

8.9   The role of education in the rescue of human intelligence.

Although IQ degeneration is a complex and multifaceted problem, education remains one of the best ways to strengthen human reasoning.

Teaching programs that encourage critical thinking, the development of problem-solving skills, and continuous learning are key to reversing this trend.

Promoting an education based on deep understanding, analysis and research is what can cultivate an intellectually healthy and resilient society.

8.10   Educational reform in Finland.

The Finnish education system, with its emphasis on critical thinking and collaboration, is a practical example of how education can foster robust cognitive skills.

Instead of a curriculum focused only on memorization and approval, the Finnish model values analytical learning, with positive results in tests of intellectual performance.

Investing in educational practices that value research, in-depth reading, and debate can be an effective way to strengthen reasoning capacity and critical thinking, preventing cognitive degeneration and promoting collective intelligence.

9   Conclusion.

Throughout this book, we have navigated the complexities of the digital age, examining the phenomena that define what we call "The Age of Stupidity." We explore the pitfalls of the infodemic, which transforms the abundance of information into disinformation; we analyze the rise of fake news and disinformation as tools of manipulation; and we discuss the challenges of technological stupidity, which reflects both the rejection of innovation and the blind acceptance of technology without critical thinking.

We also discuss the interaction between human intelligence and artificial intelligence, revealing how our cognitive limitations can be enhanced or mitigated when confronted with AI systems.

In the chapters that examined cognitive biases, such as confirmation bias and the availability heuristic, we saw how these fallacies shape our choices, often leading us to impulsive decisions or to rely on misleading information.

In addition, the book highlighted the need for a critical and ethical view in the interaction with technologies, proposing practices and approaches for a more conscious relationship with information.

This volume, therefore, sheds light on the growing complexity of our informational age, inviting the reader to a posture of reflection and responsibility.

However, this work is just the beginning of an essential journey in the field of artificial intelligence and data science. This volume is part of a larger collection, "Artificial Intelligence: The Power of Data," which explores, in depth, different aspects of AI and its implications for society and the market.

The other volumes address equally crucial topics, such as the integration of AI systems, predictive analytics, and the use of advanced algorithms for decision-making.

By purchasing and reading the other books in the collection, you will have a holistic and deep vision that will allow you not only to optimize data governance, but also to enhance the impact of artificial intelligence on your operations and understand, with greater clarity and depth, the vast digital universe that continues to redefine our lives and choices.

10 References.

ASIMOV, Isaac. I, Robot. Spectra, 1950.

B. SETTLES, Active learning literature survey, Technical Report, University of Wisconsin-Madison D partment of Computer Sciences, 2009.

BERKOVSKY, K. Yu, S. CONWAY, D. TAIB, R., ZHOU, J. and CHEN, F. (2018). Do I trust a machine? Differences in user trust based on system performance, in: Human and Machine Learning, Springer, pp. 245–264.

BERNERS-Lee, T., MANSOUR, E., SAMBRA, A., et al. (2016). A Demonstration of the Solid Platform for Social Web Applications. Published inThe Web Conference. Available at https://dl.acm.org/doi/10.1145/2872518.2890529.

BRATSBERG, Bernt; ROGEBERG, Ole. Flynn Effect and its Reversal Are Both Environmentally Caused. Proceedings of the National Academy of Sciences, 2018.

Data Management Association International (DAMA). (2020). "Data Governance Best Practices for NoSQL Databases and Graphs". DAMA White Paper Series, 7.

FLYNN, James R. Are We Getting Smarter? Rising IQ in the Twenty-First Century. Cambridge University Press, 2012.

GEVA, M., KHASHABI, D., SEGAL, E., KHOT, T., ROTH, D., & BERANT, J. (2021).

GOLEMAN, Daniel. Emotional Intelligence: Why It Can Matter More Than IQ. Bantam, 1995.

HARRIS, Tristan. The Social Dilemma. Exposure Labs, 2020.

HAWKINS, J., & BLAKESLEE, S. (2004). On Intelligence. New York: Times Books.

KAHNEMAN, Daniel. Thinking, Fast and Slow. Farrar, Straus and Giroux, 2011.

LOGAN, D. (2020). The Emergence of the Chief Data Officer. Journal of Data

O'NEIL, Cathy. Weapons of Math Destruction: How Big Data Increases Inequality and Threatens Democracy. Crown, 2016.

PARISER, Eli. The Filter Bubble: What the Internet Is Hiding from You. Penguin Press, 2011.

ROSEN, Larry. The Distracted Mind: Ancient Brains in a High-Tech World. MIT Press, 2016.

RUSSELL, Stuart; NORVIG, Peter. Artificial Intelligence: A Modern Approach. Prentice Hall, 2010.

S.A. CAMBO and D. GERGLE, User-Centred Evaluation for Machine Learning, in: Human and Machine

SUNSTEIN, Cass R. Republic: Divided Democracy in the Age of Social Media. Princeton University Press, 2017.

11 Descubra a Coleção Completa "Inteligência Artificial e o Poder dos Dados" – Um Convite para Transformar sua Carreira e Conhecimento.

A Coleção "Inteligência Artificial e o Poder dos Dados" foi criada para quem deseja não apenas entender a Inteligência Artificial (IA), mas também aplicá-la de forma estratégica e prática.

Em uma série de volumes cuidadosamente elaborados, desvendo conceitos complexos de maneira clara e acessível, garantindo ao leitor uma compreensão completa da IA e de seu impacto nas sociedades modernas.

Não importa seu nível de familiaridade com o tema: esta coleção transforma o difícil em didático, o teórico em aplicável e o técnico em algo poderoso para sua carreira.

11.1 Por Que Comprar Esta Coleção?

Estamos vivendo uma revolução tecnológica sem precedentes, onde a IA é a força motriz em áreas como medicina, finanças, educação, governo e entretenimento.

A coleção "Inteligência Artificial e o Poder dos Dados" mergulha profundamente em todos esses setores, com exemplos práticos e reflexões que vão muito além dos conceitos tradicionais.

Você encontrará tanto o conhecimento técnico quanto as implicações éticas e sociais da IA incentivando você a ver essa tecnologia não apenas como uma ferramenta, mas como um verdadeiro agente de transformação.

Cada volume é uma peça fundamental deste quebra-cabeça inovador: do aprendizado de máquina à governança de dados e da ética à aplicação prática.

Com a orientação de um autor experiente, que combina pesquisa acadêmica com anos de atuação prática, esta coleção é mais do que um conjunto de livros – é um guia indispensável para quem quer navegar e se destacar nesse campo em expansão.

11.2 Público-Alvo desta Coleção?

Esta coleção é para todos que desejam ter um papel de destaque na era da IA:

- ✓ Profissionais da Tecnologia: recebem insights técnicos profundos para expandir suas habilidades.

- ✓ Estudantes e Curiosos: têm acesso a explicações claras que facilitam o entendimento do complexo universo da IA.

- ✓ Gestores, líderes empresariais e formuladores de políticas também se beneficiarão da visão estratégica sobre a IA, essencial para a tomada de decisões bem-informadas.

- ✓ Profissionais em Transição de Carreira: Profissionais em transição de carreira ou interessados em se especializar em IA encontram aqui um material completo para construir sua trajetória de aprendizado.

11.3 Muito Mais do Que Técnica – Uma Transformação Completa.

Esta coleção não é apenas uma série de livros técnicos; é uma ferramenta de crescimento intelectual e profissional.

Com ela, você vai muito além da teoria: cada volume convida a uma reflexão profunda sobre o futuro da humanidade em um mundo onde máquinas e algoritmos estão cada vez mais presentes.

Este é o seu convite para dominar o conhecimento que vai definir o futuro e se tornar parte da transformação que a Inteligência Artificial traz ao mundo.

Seja um líder em seu setor, domine as habilidades que o mercado exige e prepare-se para o futuro com a coleção "Inteligência Artificial e o Poder dos Dados".

Esta não é apenas uma compra; é um investimento decisivo na sua jornada de aprendizado e desenvolvimento profissional.

Prof. Marcão - Marcus Vinícius Pinto

Mestre em Tecnologia da Informação.
Especialista em Inteligência Artificial, Governança de Dados e Arquitetura de Informação.

12 Os Livros da Coleção.

12.1 Dados, Informação e Conhecimento na era da Inteligência Artificial.

Este livro explora de forma essencial as bases teóricas e práticas da Inteligência Artificial, desde a coleta de dados até sua transformação em inteligência. Ele foca, principalmente, no aprendizado de máquina, no treinamento de IA e nas redes neurais.

12.2 Dos Dados em Ouro: Como Transformar Informação em Sabedoria na Era da IA.

Este livro oferece uma análise crítica sobre a evolução da Inteligência Artificial, desde os dados brutos até a criação de sabedoria artificial, integrando redes neurais, aprendizado profundo e modelagem de conhecimento.

Apresenta exemplos práticos em saúde, finanças e educação, e aborda desafios éticos e técnicos.

12.3 Desafios e Limitações dos Dados na IA.

O livro oferece uma análise profunda sobre o papel dos dados no desenvolvimento da IA explorando temas como qualidade, viés, privacidade, segurança e escalabilidade com estudos de caso práticos em saúde, finanças e segurança pública.

12.4 Dados Históricos em Bases de Dados para IA: Estruturas, Preservação e Expurgo.

Este livro investiga como a gestão de dados históricos é essencial para o sucesso de projetos de IA. Aborda a relevância das normas ISO para garantir qualidade e segurança, além de analisar tendências e inovações no tratamento de dados.

12.5   Vocabulário Controlado para Dicionário de Dados: Um Guia Completo.

Este guia completo explora as vantagens e desafios da implementação de vocabulários controlados no contexto da IA e da ciência da informação. Com uma abordagem detalhada, aborda desde a nomeação de elementos de dados até as interações entre semântica e cognição.

12.6   Curadoria e Administração de Dados para a Era da IA.

Esta obra apresenta estratégias avançadas para transformar dados brutos em insights valiosos, com foco na curadoria meticulosa e administração eficiente dos dados. Além de soluções técnicas, aborda questões éticas e legais, capacitando o leitor a enfrentar os desafios complexos da informação.

12.7   Arquitetura de Informação.

A obra aborda a gestão de dados na era digital, combinando teoria e prática para criar sistemas de IA eficientes e escaláveis, com insights sobre modelagem e desafios éticos e legais.

12.8   Fundamentos: O Essencial para Dominar a Inteligência Artificial.

Uma obra essencial para quem deseja dominar os conceitos-chave da IA, com uma abordagem acessível e exemplos práticos. O livro explora inovações como Machine Learning e Processamento de Linguagem Natural, além dos desafios éticos e legais e oferece uma visão clara do impacto da IA em diversos setores.

12.9   LLMS - Modelos de Linguagem de Grande Escala.

Este guia essencial ajuda a compreender a revolução dos Modelos de Linguagem de Grande Escala (LLMs) na IA.

O livro explora a evolução dos GPTs e as últimas inovações em interação humano-computador, oferecendo insights práticos sobre seu impacto em setores como saúde, educação e finanças.

12.10 Machine Learning: Fundamentos e Avanços.

Este livro oferece uma visão abrangente sobre algoritmos supervisionados e não supervisionados, redes neurais profundas e aprendizado federado. Além de abordar questões de ética e explicabilidade dos modelos.

12.11 Por Dentro das Mentes Sintéticas.

Este livro revela como essas 'mentes sintéticas' estão redefinindo a criatividade, o trabalho e as interações humanas. Esta obra apresenta uma análise detalhada dos desafios e oportunidades proporcionados por essas tecnologias, explorando seu impacto profundo na sociedade.

12.12 A Questão dos Direitos Autorais.

Este livro convida o leitor a explorar o futuro da criatividade em um mundo onde a colaboração entre humanos e máquinas é uma realidade, abordando questões sobre autoria, originalidade e propriedade intelectual na era das IAs generativas.

12.13 1121 Perguntas e Respostas: Do Básico ao Complexo– Parte 1 A 4.

Organizadas em quatro volumes, estas perguntas servem como guias práticos essenciais para dominar os principais conceitos da IA.

A Parte 1 aborda informação, dados, geoprocessamento, a evolução da inteligência artificial, seus marcos históricos e conceitos básicos.

A Parte 2 aprofunda-se em conceitos complexos como aprendizado de máquina, processamento de linguagem natural, visão computacional, robótica e algoritmos de decisão.

A Parte 3 aborda questões como privacidade de dados, automação do trabalho e o impacto de modelos de linguagem de grande escala (LLMs).

Parte 4 explora o papel central dos dados na era da inteligência artificial, aprofundando os fundamentos da IA e suas aplicações em áreas como saúde mental, governo e combate à corrupção.

12.14 O Glossário Definitivo da Inteligência Artificial.

Este glossário apresenta mais de mil conceitos de inteligência artificial explicados de forma clara, abordando temas como Machine Learning, Processamento de Linguagem Natural, Visão Computacional e Ética em IA.

- A parte 1 contempla conceitos iniciados pelas letras de A a D.
- A parte 2 contempla conceitos iniciados pelas letras de E a M.
- A parte 3 contempla conceitos iniciados pelas letras de N a Z.

12.15 Engenharia de Prompt - Volumes 1 a 6.

Esta coleção abrange todos os fundamentos da engenharia de prompt, proporcionando uma base completa para o desenvolvimento profissional.

Com uma rica variedade de prompts para áreas como liderança, marketing digital e tecnologia da informação, oferece exemplos práticos para melhorar a clareza, a tomada de decisões e obter insights valiosos.

Os volumes abordam os seguintes assuntos:

- Volume 1: Fundamentos. Conceitos Estruturadores e História da Engenharia de Prompt.
- Volume 2: Segurança e Privacidade em IA.
- Volume 3: Modelos de Linguagem, Tokenização e Métodos de Treinamento.
- Volume 4: Como Fazer Perguntas Corretas.
- Volume 5: Estudos de Casos e Erros.
- Volume 6: Os Melhores Prompts.

12.16 Guia para ser um Engenheiro De Prompt – Volumes 1 e 2.

A coleção explora os fundamentos avançados e as habilidades necessárias para ser um engenheiro de prompt bem-sucedido, destacando os benefícios, riscos e o papel crítico que essa função desempenha no desenvolvimento da inteligência artificial.

O Volume 1 aborda a elaboração de prompts eficazes, enquanto o Volume 2 é um guia para compreender e aplicar os fundamentos da Engenharia de Prompt.

12.17 Governança de Dados com IA – Volumes 1 a 3.

Descubra como implementar uma governança de dados eficaz com esta coleção abrangente. Oferecendo orientações práticas, esta coleção abrange desde a arquitetura e organização de dados até a proteção e garantia de qualidade, proporcionando uma visão completa para transformar dados em ativos estratégicos.

O volume 1 aborda as práticas e regulações. O volume 2 explora em profundidade os processos, técnicas e melhores práticas para realizar auditorias eficazes em modelos de dados. O volume 3 é seu guia definitivo para implantação da governança de dados com IA.

12.18 Governança de Algoritmos.

Este livro analisa o impacto dos algoritmos na sociedade, explorando seus fundamentos e abordando questões éticas e regulatórias. Aborda transparência, accountability e vieses, com soluções práticas para auditar e monitorar algoritmos em setores como finanças, saúde e educação.

12.19 De Profissional de Ti para Expert em IA: O Guia Definitivo para uma Transição de Carreira Bem-Sucedida.

Para profissionais de Tecnologia da Informação, a transição para a IA representa uma oportunidade única de aprimorar habilidades e contribuir para o desenvolvimento de soluções inovadoras que moldam o futuro.

Neste livro, investigamos os motivos para fazer essa transição, as habilidades essenciais, a melhor trilha de aprendizado e as perspectivas para o futuro do mercado de trabalho em TI.

12.20 Liderança Inteligente com IA: Transforme sua Equipe e Impulsione Resultados.

Este livro revela como a inteligência artificial pode revolucionar a gestão de equipes e maximizar o desempenho organizacional.

Combinando técnicas de liderança tradicionais com insights proporcionados pela IA, como a liderança baseada em análise preditiva, você aprenderá a otimizar processos, tomar decisões mais estratégicas e criar equipes mais eficientes e engajadas.

12.21 Impactos e Transformações: Coleção Completa.

Esta coleção oferece uma análise abrangente e multifacetada das transformações provocadas pela Inteligência Artificial na sociedade contemporânea.

- Volume 1: Desafios e Soluções na Detecção de Textos Gerados por Inteligência Artificial.
- Volume 2: A Era das Bolhas de Filtro. Inteligência Artificial e a Ilusão de Liberdade.
- Volume 3: Criação de Conteúdo com IA - Como Fazer?
- Volume 4: A Singularidade Está Mais Próxima do que Você Imagina.
- Volume 5: Burrice Humana versus Inteligência Artificial.
- Volume 6: A Era da Burrice! Um Culto à Estupidez?
- Volume 7: Autonomia em Movimento: A Revolução dos Veículos Inteligentes.
- Volume 8: Poiesis e Criatividade com IA.
- Volume 9: Dupla perfeita: IA + automação.
- Volume 10: Quem detém o poder dos dados?

12.22 Big Data com IA: Coleção Completa.

A coleção aborda desde os fundamentos tecnológicos e a arquitetura de Big Data até a administração e o glossário de termos técnicos essenciais.

A coleção também discute o futuro da relação da humanidade com o enorme volume de dados gerados nas bases de dados de treinamento em estruturação de Big Data.

- Volume 1: Fundamentos.
- Volume 2: Arquitetura.
- Volume 3: Implementação.
- Volume 4: Administração.
- Volume 5: Temas Essenciais e Definições.
- Volume 6: Data Warehouse, Big Data e IA.

13 Sobre o Autor.

Sou Marcus Pinto, mais conhecido como Prof. Marcão, especialista em tecnologia da informação, arquitetura da informação e inteligência artificial.

Com mais de quatro décadas de atuação e pesquisa dedicadas, construí uma trajetória sólida e reconhecida, sempre focada em tornar o conhecimento técnico acessível e aplicável a todos os que buscam entender e se destacar nesse campo transformador.

Minha experiência abrange consultoria estratégica, educação e autoria, além de uma atuação extensa como analista de arquitetura de informação.

Essa vivência me capacita a oferecer soluções inovadoras e adaptadas às necessidades em constante evolução do mercado tecnológico, antecipando tendências e criando pontes entre o saber técnico e o impacto prático.

Ao longo dos anos, desenvolvi uma expertise abrangente e aprofundada em dados, inteligência artificial e governança da informação – áreas que se tornaram essenciais para a construção de sistemas robustos e seguros, capazes de lidar com o vasto volume de dados que molda o mundo atual.

Minha coleção de livros, disponível na Amazon, reflete essa expertise, abordando temas como Governança de Dados, Big Data e Inteligência Artificial com um enfoque claro em aplicações práticas e visão estratégica.

Autor de mais de 150 livros, investigo o impacto da inteligência artificial em múltiplas esferas, explorando desde suas bases técnicas até as questões éticas que se tornam cada vez mais urgentes com a adoção dessa tecnologia em larga escala.

Em minhas palestras e mentorias, compartilho não apenas o valor da IA, mas também os desafios e responsabilidades que acompanham sua implementação – elementos que considero essenciais para uma adoção ética e consciente.

Acredito que a evolução tecnológica é um caminho inevitável. Meus livros são uma proposta de guia nesse trajeto, oferecendo insights profundos e acessíveis para quem deseja não apenas entender, mas dominar as tecnologias do futuro.

Com um olhar focado na educação e no desenvolvimento humano, convido você a se unir a mim nessa jornada transformadora, explorando as possibilidades e desafios que essa era digital nos reserva.

14 Como Contatar o Prof. Marcão.

14.1 Para palestras, treinamento e mentoria empresarial.

marcao.tecno@gmail.com

14.2 Prof. Marcão, no Linkedin.

https://bit.ly/linkedin_profmarcao

www.ingramcontent.com/pod-product-compliance
Lightning Source LLC
Chambersburg PA
CBHW061052050326
40690CB00012B/2591